To Do

- ◯
- ◯
- ◯
- ◯
- ◯
- ◯
- ◯
- ◯
- ◯
- ◯
- ◯
- ◯
- ◯

Notes

TODAY'S DATE: _______________

AM		PM	
5:00		1:00	
6:00		2:00	
7:00		3:00	
8:00		4:00	
9:00		5:00	
10:00		6:00	
11:00		7:00	
12:00		8:00	

POCKET AGENDA BOOK

---

for

BUSY PEOPLE

Speedy Publishing LLC
40 E. Main St., #1156
Newark, DE 19711

www.SpeedyPublishing.Co

Today's Date: _______________________

AM		PM	
5:00		**1:00**	
6:00		**2:00**	
7:00		**3:00**	
8:00		**4:00**	
9:00		**5:00**	
10:00		**6:00**	
11:00		**7:00**	
12:00		**8:00**	

To Do

Notes

Today's Date: __________

AM		PM	
5:00		**1:00**	
6:00		**2:00**	
7:00		**3:00**	
8:00		**4:00**	
9:00		**5:00**	
10:00		**6:00**	
11:00		**7:00**	
12:00		**8:00**	

To Do

- ○
- ○
- ○
- ○
- ○
- ○
- ○
- ○
- ○
- ○
- ○
- ○
- ○

Notes

TODAY'S DATE: ________________________

AM		PM	
5:00		**1:00**	
6:00		**2:00**	
7:00		**3:00**	
8:00		**4:00**	
9:00		**5:00**	
10:00		**6:00**	
11:00		**7:00**	
12:00		**8:00**	

To Do

Notes

AM		PM	
5:00		1:00	
6:00		2:00	
7:00		3:00	
8:00		4:00	
9:00		5:00	
10:00		6:00	
11:00		7:00	
12:00		8:00	

To Do

Notes

TODAY'S DATE: _______________________

	AM		PM
5:00		1:00	
6:00		2:00	
7:00		3:00	
8:00		4:00	
9:00		5:00	
10:00		6:00	
11:00		7:00	
12:00		8:00	

To Do

Notes

TODAY'S DATE: _______________________

AM		PM	
5:00		**1:00**	
6:00		**2:00**	
7:00		**3:00**	
8:00		**4:00**	
9:00		**5:00**	
10:00		**6:00**	
11:00		**7:00**	
12:00		**8:00**	

To Do

Notes

Today's Date: ________________________

AM		PM	
5:00		1:00	
6:00		2:00	
7:00		3:00	
8:00		4:00	
9:00		5:00	
10:00		6:00	
11:00		7:00	
12:00		8:00	

To Do

-
-
-
-
-
-
-
-
-
-
-
-
-

Notes

TODAY'S DATE: _______________________

AM		PM	
5:00		**1:00**	
6:00		**2:00**	
7:00		**3:00**	
8:00		**4:00**	
9:00		**5:00**	
10:00		**6:00**	
11:00		**7:00**	
12:00		**8:00**	

To Do

- ◯ ____
- ◯ ____
- ◯ ____
- ◯ ____
- ◯ ____
- ◯ ____
- ◯ ____
- ◯ ____
- ◯ ____
- ◯ ____
- ◯ ____
- ◯ ____
- ◯ ____
- ◯ ____

Notes

____

____

____

____

TODAY'S DATE: _______________________________

AM		PM	
5:00		1:00	
6:00		2:00	
7:00		3:00	
8:00		4:00	
9:00		5:00	
10:00		6:00	
11:00		7:00	
12:00		8:00	

To Do

Notes

Today's Date: _______________________

AM		PM	
5:00		1:00	
6:00		2:00	
7:00		3:00	
8:00		4:00	
9:00		5:00	
10:00		6:00	
11:00		7:00	
12:00		8:00	

To Do

- ◯
- ◯
- ◯
- ◯
- ◯
- ◯
- ◯
- ◯
- ◯
- ◯
- ◯
- ◯
- ◯

Notes

Today's Date: _______________

AM		PM	
5:00		**1:00**	
6:00		**2:00**	
7:00		**3:00**	
8:00		**4:00**	
9:00		**5:00**	
10:00		**6:00**	
11:00		**7:00**	
12:00		**8:00**	

To Do

Notes

TODAY'S DATE: ______________________________

AM		PM	
5:00		**1:00**	
6:00		**2:00**	
7:00		**3:00**	
8:00		**4:00**	
9:00		**5:00**	
10:00		**6:00**	
11:00		**7:00**	
12:00		**8:00**	

To Do

Notes

Today's Date: ________________

AM		PM	
5:00		**1:00**	
6:00		**2:00**	
7:00		**3:00**	
8:00		**4:00**	
9:00		**5:00**	
10:00		**6:00**	
11:00		**7:00**	
12:00		**8:00**	

To Do

Notes

TODAY'S DATE: ______________________

AM		PM	
5:00		1:00	
6:00		2:00	
7:00		3:00	
8:00		4:00	
9:00		5:00	
10:00		6:00	
11:00		7:00	
12:00		8:00	

To Do

Notes

Today's Date: ___________________

AM		PM	
5:00		1:00	
6:00		2:00	
7:00		3:00	
8:00		4:00	
9:00		5:00	
10:00		6:00	
11:00		7:00	
12:00		8:00	

To Do

Notes

TODAY'S DATE: ________________

AM		PM	
5:00		**1:00**	
6:00		**2:00**	
7:00		**3:00**	
8:00		**4:00**	
9:00		**5:00**	
10:00		**6:00**	
11:00		**7:00**	
12:00		**8:00**	

To Do

Notes

TODAY'S DATE: ______________________

AM		PM	
5:00		1:00	
6:00		2:00	
7:00		3:00	
8:00		4:00	
9:00		5:00	
10:00		6:00	
11:00		7:00	
12:00		8:00	

To Do

- ○ _______________________________________
- ○ _______________________________________
- ○ _______________________________________
- ○ _______________________________________
- ○ _______________________________________
- ○ _______________________________________
- ○ _______________________________________
- ○ _______________________________________
- ○ _______________________________________
- ○ _______________________________________
- ○ _______________________________________
- ○ _______________________________________
- ○ _______________________________________
- ○ _______________________________________

Notes

____

____

____

____

____

Today's Date: ______________________

AM		PM	
5:00		**1:00**	
6:00		**2:00**	
7:00		**3:00**	
8:00		**4:00**	
9:00		**5:00**	
10:00		**6:00**	
11:00		**7:00**	
12:00		**8:00**	

To Do

Notes

Today's Date: _______________________

AM		PM	
5:00		1:00	
6:00		2:00	
7:00		3:00	
8:00		4:00	
9:00		5:00	
10:00		6:00	
11:00		7:00	
12:00		8:00	

To Do

Notes

TODAY'S DATE: _______________________

AM	PM
5:00	1:00
6:00	2:00
7:00	3:00
8:00	4:00
9:00	5:00
10:00	6:00
11:00	7:00
12:00	8:00

To Do

- [ ]
- [ ]
- [ ]
- [ ]
- [ ]
- [ ]
- [ ]
- [ ]
- [ ]
- [ ]
- [ ]
- [ ]
- [ ]

Notes

TODAY'S DATE: _______________________

AM		PM	
5:00		**1:00**	
6:00		**2:00**	
7:00		**3:00**	
8:00		**4:00**	
9:00		**5:00**	
10:00		**6:00**	
11:00		**7:00**	
12:00		**8:00**	

To Do

Notes

Today's Date: _______________________

AM		PM	
5:00		1:00	
6:00		2:00	
7:00		3:00	
8:00		4:00	
9:00		5:00	
10:00		6:00	
11:00		7:00	
12:00		8:00	

To Do

Notes

TODAY'S DATE: ____________________

AM		PM	
5:00		**1:00**	
6:00		**2:00**	
7:00		**3:00**	
8:00		**4:00**	
9:00		**5:00**	
10:00		**6:00**	
11:00		**7:00**	
12:00		**8:00**	

To Do

- ○
- ○
- ○
- ○
- ○
- ○
- ○
- ○
- ○
- ○
- ○
- ○
- ○

Notes